asian **resorts**

complejos turísticos asiáticos

complessi turistici in asia

© 2003 Feierabend Verlag OHG
Mommsenstr. 43
D- 10629 Berlin

Traducción del inglés: Silvia Gómez de Antonio & Irene Moreno Palacios
Traduzione dall' inglese: Raffaella Durante-Müller & Eleonora Zoratti
Typesetting of the trilingual edition: adHOC Laureck & Beuster oHG

Author: Tan Hock Beng
Photographer: Tan Hock Beng (unless otherwise stated)

Editorial director: Kelley Cheng
Art director: Jacinta Neoh
Sub-editors/writers: Hwee-Chuin Ang & Narelle Yakuba
Graphic designers : Chai-Yen Wong & Sharn Selina Lim

Colour separation: SC Graphic Technology Pte Ltd

Asian Resorts
First published in Singapore in 2003
by Page One Publishing Private Limited
Text & Photography © copyright 2003 Page One Publishing Private Limited

Printing and Binding: Stampa Nazionale s.r.l., Italy

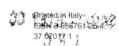
Printed in Italy
ISBN 3-936761-26-4
37 070 17 1

asian **resorts**

complejos turísticos asiáticos

complessi turistici in asia

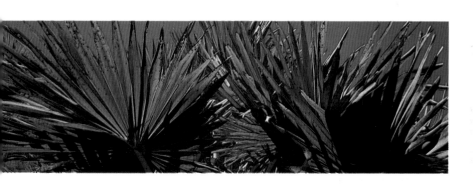

Feierabend

contents
sumario
sommario

contents
sumario
sommario

introduction
introducción
introduzione

The resort industry of tropical Asia has produced one of the most vibrant architectural scenes in the world. Not only is Asia one of the culturally richest regions in the world, it has also exceptional landscapes and stunning natural features – factors that have made the region a major tourist destination. Well-designed resorts of simple materiality, consummate craftsmanship, and rich moods are pervasive. Inspired by a reverence for the tropical climate, the rich cultural heritage as well as the pristine sites, these buildings demonstrate a poetic understanding and keen appreciation of natural and cultural determinants. The blend of design trends like Minimalism incorporating abstracted elements of traditional design has resulted in a particular style that has both global and local appeal. The tourism industry has successfully constructed a new niche by marketing the «concept of authenticity» which offers tourists a more «culturally sensitive» and «politically correct» form of travel accommodation. Architects of these stylish works have produced an architectural ensemble that possesses a sensual refinement and a sure sense of place. The concept of luxury is redefined through a sense of tactility and tranquility. Resorts are unique juxtapositions of landscape and architecture – of empathy and resonance – anchoring their inhabitants and visitors firmly to the poetics of a place.

The contents of the book is meant to showcase both traditional architecture and contemporary projects that have drawn inspiration from the past. The intention is not to provide a comprehensive guide to architecture in Southeast Asia, but to present selective samples, and, at the same time, to ensure that the aura of the tropics can be felt by choosing a sufficient range of buildings. A cursory view offers endless delight to the reader.

Tan Hock Beng | Singapore, September 2002

La industria turística del Asia tropical ha creado uno de los escenarios arquitectónicos más vibrantes del mundo. Asia no es sólo una de las regiones culturales más ricas del mundo, sino que también posee unos paisajes excepcionales además de sorprendentes características naturales. Estos factores han contribuido a que esta región se convierta en uno de los destinos turísticos más importantes. Los complejos turísticos, de magnífico diseño y construidos a partir de materiales sencillos, la destreza consumada y la riqueza de los ambientes lo invaden todo. Inspirados por un profundo respeto hacia el clima tropical, por el rico patrimonio cultural y por los lugares prístinos, estos edificios demuestran una poética comprensión además de una profunda apreciación de los factores naturales y culturales. De la combinación de diferentes tendencias artísticas, como el minimalismo, y la incorporación de elementos abstractos del diseño tradicional, ha surgido un estilo propio que incluye encantos tanto particulares como mundiales. La industria del turismo ha construido con éxito un nuevo nicho comercializando con el «concepto de autenticidad», que ofrece a los turistas un tipo de alojamiento turístico más «sensible culturalmente» y «políticamente correcto». Los arquitectos de esta obra rebosante de estilo han creado un conjunto arquitectónico que posee una delicadeza sensual y una clara percepción del lugar. El concepto de lujo se redefine gracias a un sentido lleno de tacto y tranquilidad. Los centros turísticos son yuxtaposiciones únicas de paisaje y arquitectura, de empatía y resonancia, anclando firmemente a sus habitantes y visitantes en la poética del lugar. El contenido de esta obra quiere ser un escaparate tanto de la arquitectura tradicional como de los proyectos contemporáneos que se han inspirado en el pasado. La intención de este libro no es suministrar una guía completa de la arquitectura del sudeste asiático, sino presentar unos ejemplos selectivos y procurar, al mismo tiempo, que el aura de los trópicos pueda sentirse a partir de una amplia selección de edificios. Una visión general le ofrece al lector un deleite interminable.

Tan Hock Beng | Singapur, septiembre de 2002

Le residenze private e i complessi turistici dell'Asia tropicale offrono scenari architettonici tra i più vivaci al mondo. L'Asia non è infatti solo una delle regioni culturalmente più ricche, ma presenta anche paesaggi straordinari e bellezze naturali indimenticabili; questo ha fatto della regione una meta turistica tra le più ambite. Residenze e complessi alberghieri sono attentamente progettati, costruiti con materiali semplici, manodopera artigianale e coinvolgimento emotivo. Ispirati dal rispetto per il clima tropicale, il ricco patrimonio culturale e i siti archeologici, questi edifici rivelano una comprensione poetica e un profondo apprezzamento dei fattori naturali e culturali. La fusione di tendenze di design come il minimalismo con elementi astratti di ispirazione tradizionale ha prodotto uno stile unico che fonde il fascino locale e globale al tempo stesso. Il settore turistico è riuscito a creare una nuova nicchia promuovendo il concetto di «autenticità» che offre ai turisti una forma di alloggio culturalmente più sensibile e «politicamente corretta». Gli architetti di questi gioielli di stile hanno prodotto insiemi architettonici contraddistinti da una raffinata sensualità e da una profonda conoscenza del luogo. Il concetto di lusso è corretto e ridefinito dalla concretezza delle sensazioni tattili e dalla tranquillità. Questi edifici nascono da una giustapposizione unica di paesaggio e di architettura, di empatia e di risonanza, ancorando saldamente abitanti e visitatori alla poetica del luogo.

Le immagini mostrano sia esempi di architettura tradizionale che progetti contemporanei ispirati al passato. L'intenzione non è quella di fornire una guida completa all'architettura nell'Asia sudoccidentale, ma di presentarne esempi selezionati e, allo stesso tempo, di trasmettere il fascino dei tropici grazie alla presentazione di una varietà di edifici. Una visione d'insieme offre al lettore la gioia di ammirare queste bellezze architettoniche.

Tan Hock Beng | Singapore, settembre 2002

COMPOSITION

forms and facades

The tropical house is characterised by courtyards, verandahs, pitched roofs with deep-overhangs, prevalent use of timber and a concern for shade and cross-ventilation.

COMPOSICIÓN

formas y fachadas

La casa tropical se caracteriza por sus jardines interiores, sus verandas, sus tejados inclinados con profundos salientes, el uso predominante de la madera y una preocupación por la sombra y la ventilación cruzada.

COMPOSIZIONE

forme e facciate

La casa tropicale è caratterizzata da cortili, verande, tetti a spiovente con pronunciate sporgenze, un uso dominante del legno e la necessità di creare ombra e ventilazione.

Traditional architecture arose from the needs and relationships of man with society and environment. Southeast Asia has long developed its unique identity and is one of the most culturally rich areas of the world. The hot and wet climate has shaped its culture, and consequentially, its built-forms. Climatic factors are the mainspring of the sensual qualities that make up tropical architecture. The tropical house is characterised by courtyards, verandahs, pitched roofs with deep overhangs, prevalent use of timber and a concern for shade and cross-ventilation.

In tropical architecture, semi-permeable walls maximise the interface between the interior and the exterior. Instead of isolating the occupants from the external environment, semi-permeable walls offer immediate contact with the surroundings. High ceilings also encourage the free flow of air. These delightful qualities are triggers to the local collective memory. The rise of the resort industry has spawned a number of progenies that not only exhibit these qualities, but also recombine elements from the past with those from another source outside its cultural context.

La arquitectura tradicional surgió de las obligaciones y relaciones del hombre con la sociedad y el medio. El sudeste asiático ha desarrollado durante largo tiempo su identidad única y es una de las áreas culturales más ricas de todo el mundo. El clima cálido y húmedo ha conformado su cultura y, consecuentemente, sus construcciones. Los factores climáticos son los motivos principales de las sensuales características que conforman la arquitectura tropical. La casa tropical se caracteriza por los jardines, las verandas, los tejados inclinados con profundos salientes, el uso predominante de la madera y la preocupación por la sombra y la ventilación cruzada.

En la arquitectura tropical, las paredes semipermeables maximizan las zonas de contacto entre el interior y el exterior. En vez de aislar a los ocupantes del medio exterior, los muros semipermeables permiten un contacto más directo con el entorno. Los techos altos también facilitan la libre circulación del aire. Estas encantadoras características son recuerdos que despiertan la memoria colectiva local. El crecimiento de la industria del turismo ha dado lugar en la arquitectura a una serie de generaciones posteriores que no sólo presentan estas características, sino que además fusionan elementos del pasado con otros ajenos a su contexto cultural.

L'architettura tradizionale è sorta dai bisogni dell'uomo e dalla sua relazione con la società e con l'ambiente. L'Asia sudoccidentale ha sviluppato per un periodo lunghissimo di tempo la sua identità del tutto unica ed è una delle zone culturalmente più ricche al mondo. Il clima caldo e umido ha formato la sua cultura e con essa le forme architettoniche. I fattori climatici sono il fattore principale della sensualità evidente nell'architettura tropicale. La casa tropicale è caratterizzata da cortili, verande, tetti a spiovente con pronunciate sporgenze, un uso dominante del legno e la necessità di creare ombra e ventilazione.

Pareti semipermeabili potenziano il ruolo degli elementi di connessione tra interni ed esterni. Anziché isolare gli abitanti dall'ambiente esterno, le pareti semipermeabili permettono un contatto immediato con l'ambiente circostante; gli alti soffitti favoriscono inoltre il passaggio dell'aria. Queste gradevoli qualità sono stimoli che attivano la memoria locale collettiva. L'affermazione del settore turistico ha dato vita a forme architettoniche che conservano i caratteri tradizionali combinandoli con elementi tratti da fonti esterne al loro contesto culturale.

«Some houses are mute,
some shout. Others sing,
and we behold their
song.»

- Christian Norberg Schulz

«Algunas casas son
mudas, algunas gritan.
Otras cantan, y nosotros
contemplamos su
canción.»

- Christian Norberg Schulz

«Alcune case sono mute,
alcune gridano. Altre
invece cantano, e noi
ascoltiamo, ammirati,
la loro canzone.»

- Christian Norberg Schulz

The precise geometric form of The Serai, Bali,
Indonesia is a fine balance between tradition
and modernity.

La precisa forma geométrica del Serai, Bali,
Indonesia, logra un magnífico equilibrio entre la
tradición y la modernidad.

La precisa forma geometrica di The Serai a Bali
in Indonesia, è il frutto di un sottile equilibrio tra
tradizione e modernità.

This traditional palace in India is a result of wonderful proportions and composition of roof forms.

Este palacio tradicional en la India es el resultado de maravillosas proporciones y de la composición de las formas de los tejados.

Il segreto di questo palazzo tradizionale è il tetto, con le meravigliose proporzioni e la composizione delle forme.

(**all**) Various silhouettes of the Asian roof form.
(**todo**) Varios perfiles de los diferentes tipos de tejados asiáticos.
(**tutte le foto**) Vari profili della forma tipicamente asiatica del tetto.

A cantilevered gable roof at Club Med Maldives.
Tejado voladizo de dos aguas en el Club Med Maldives.
Tetto a due falde con trave a sbalzo, Club Med Maldive.

EXPRESSION

tropical roofscape

The roof is one of the most critical determinants of form. It gives distinction and interest, and provides indelible impressions of regional characteristics.

EXPRESIÓN

tejados tropicales

El tejado es uno de los elementos más importantes que determinan la forma. Confiere distinción y atrae el interés, y ofrece impresiones imborrables de las características regionales.

ESPRESSIONE

tetto tropicale

Il tetto è uno dei fattori fondamentali della forma. Conferisce carattere e fascino e crea un'impressione indelebile delle caratteristiche regionali.

A dominant feature in Southeast Asian architecture, the roof provides shelter and gives the inhabitants a fundamental sense of security, territory and symbolic identity. In Southeast Asian societies, the house and roof are seen as animate entities. Elaborate carvings on the roof inspired by the rich myths and symbols of the culture imbue phenomenological significance to the meeting of the roof with the sky. The roof is one of the most critical determinants of form. It gives distinction and interest, and provides indelible impressions of regional characteristics. It also reflects the scope and use of a building.

Many contemporary architects advocate an approach based on using elements from vernacular tropes and combining them in new ways. They have expressed in the silhouettes of their work a sense of the poetics of the tropics, and a sincere search for new expressions that will truly enhance the places they occupy.

El tejado, rasgo importante en la arquitectura del sudeste asiático, no sólo proporciona refugio, sino que además da a los habitantes un sentimiento de seguridad, territorialidad e identidad simbólica. En las sociedades del sudeste asiático, la casa y el tejado están considerados como entidades animadas. Las elaboradas esculturas sobre los tejados, inspiradas en la rica mitología y en los símbolos de la cultura, impregnan de significado fenomenológico el encuentro entre el tejado y el cielo. El tejado es uno de los elementos más importantes que determinan la forma. Confiere distinción y atrae el interés, y ofrece impresiones imborrables de las características regionales. También refleja la importancia y el uso de un edificio.

Muchos arquitectos contemporáneos abogan por un enfoque basado en el uso de tropos vernáculos pero combinándolos de nuevas maneras. A través de las siluetas de sus obras, expresan una sensación de la poética de los trópicos y una búsqueda sincera de nuevas experiencias que verdaderamente engrandecen los lugares en los que estas construcciones se han levantado.

Fattore dominante nell'architettura dell'Asia sudoccidentale, il tetto offre rifugio e dà agli abitanti un senso di sicurezza e di identità territoriale e simbolica. Nelle società asiatiche sudoccidentali la casa e il tetto sono viste come entità animate. Elaborate incisioni sul tetto ispirate dalla ricca mitologia e simbologia locali conferiscono una valenza fenomenologica all'incontro tra il tetto e il cielo.

Il tetto è uno dei fattori fondamentali della forma. Conferisce carattere e fascino e crea un'impressione indelebile delle caratteristiche regionali. Riflette inoltre lo scopo e la funzione di un edificio.

Molti architetti contemporanei hanno scelto un approccio basato sugli elementi di località tropicali combinati in maniere nuove. Hanno espresso nei profili delle loro opere un senso della poetica dei tropici e una sincera ricerca di nuovi percorsi espressivi in grado di promuovere la bellezza dei luoghi in cui sorgono.

A guest pavilion at the Amanpuri, Phuket, Thailand.
Un pabellón de invitados en el Amanpuri, Phuket, Tailandia.
Padiglione degli ospiti all'Amanpuri Resort, Phuket, Thailandia.

A private villa, Amandari, Bali, Indonesia
Una villa particular, Armandari, Bali, Indonesia.
Villa privata, Amandari, Indonesia.

«One unchanging element of all buildings is the roof – protective, emphatic, and all-important... Ubiquitous, pervasively present, the scale or pattern shaped by the building beneath. The roof – its shape, texture and proportion - is the strongest visual factor.»

- Geoffrey Bawa

«Un elemento invariable en todos los edificios es el tejado, protector, enfático y fundamental...Ubicuo, omnipresente, las proporciones o el dibujo determinados por la planta del edificio. El tejado – su forma, textura y proporción – es el factor visual más fuerte.»

- Geoffrey Bawa

«L'elemento invariabile di un edificio è il tetto: protegge, sottolinea e domina. Ubiquitario, pervasivo, le dimensioni e la forma sono condizionate dalla costruzione che copre. Il tetto, con la sua forma, i materiali e la composizione, è il fattore visivo principale.»

- Geoffrey Bawa

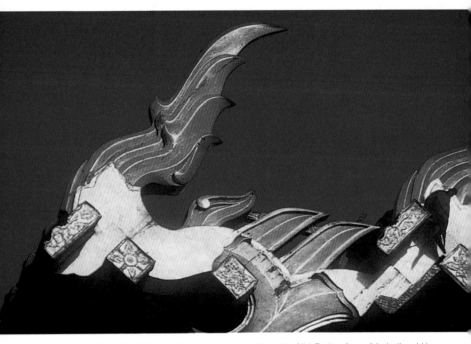

(left and right) The bargeboards at the gable ends of this Thai roof are gilded wth gold leaves.

(todo) Los pináculos al final del gablete de este tejado tailandés se han dorado con hojas de oro.

(tutte le foto) Le punte del frontone di questo tetto thailandese sono ricoperte d'oro.

INTERMISSION

transition spaces

Spaces flow from the interiors to the exteriors in an almost seamless manner, creating interesting intermediate thresholds and domains.

INTERMEDIO

espacios de transición

Los espacios fluyen desde el interior hacia el exterior de forma casi siempre ininterrumpida, creando interesantes umbrales y zonas intermedias.

INTERVALLO

spazi di transizione

Gli spazi scorrono dall'interno all'esterno in un percorso senza punti di sutura, attirando l'attenzione su soglie e settori intermedi.

The richness of a building in a tropical region is derived from the constant phenomenological awareness of the interior and the exterior. Tropical living actually occurs in this «in-between» realm – the ambiguous edge between inside and outside, private and public, shadow and light. The in-between realm has always been a critical element in the vocabulary of spatial forms in most parts of Asia.

Architecture can be perceived as an inhabited art – a space-making activity in ight, where the solid is servant to the void. This void is manifested through layered spaces, as well as transition spaces, which form an important part of the tropical consciousness. They allow for a simultaneous perception of other spatial boundaries.

In traditional Southeast Asian architecture, transparency is achieved without excluding privacy and enclosure. Interposing elements accentuate distance and difference. Filtering and transitional elements, like walls, gateways, steps and thresholds, are delightful architectural elements found in the rich traditional architecture of the region. Handled with grace, they help spaces to flow from the interiors to the exteriors in a seamless manner, creating interesting thresholds and intermediate domains.

La riqueza de un edificio en los trópicos se deriva de una conciencia fenomenológica del interior y del exterior. Realmente, la vida en los trópicos se desarrolla en este espacio «intermedio»: el límite ambiguo entre dentro y fuera, privado y público, sombra y luz. En la mayor parte de Asia, el espacio intermedio ha sido siempre un elemento muy importante en el vocabulario de las formas espaciales.

La arquitectura puede ser percibida como un arte habitado, una actividad que crea espacios en la luz, donde la materia está al servicio del vacío. Este vacío se manifiesta a través de espacios estratificados y espacios de transición, que constituyen una parte importante de la conciencia tropical. Permiten una percepción simultánea de otros límites espaciales.

En la arquitectura tradicional del sudeste asiático, la transparencia se consigue sin excluir la privacidad y los recintos cerrados. La interposición de los elementos acentúa la distancia y la diferencia. Los elementos filtrantes y de transición, como paredes, puertas, peldaños y umbrales, son fascinantes elementos arquitectónicos que se encuentran en la rica tradición arquitectónica de la región. Dispuestos con habilidad, contribuyen a que los espacios fluyan desde el interior al exterior de forma continua, creando umbrales y zonas intermedias fascinantes.

La ricchezza di un edificio nei tropici deriva dalla consapevolezza fenomenologica costante del rapporto tra interno ed esterno. La vita ai tropici si svolge di fatto in questo regno «di mezzo», sull'ambiguo confine tra dentro e fuori, privato e pubblico, luce e ombra. Il regno «di mezzo» è sempre stato un elemento fondamentale nel vocabolario delle forme spaziali in quasi tutta l'Asia.

L'architettura può essere vista come arte abitata, un'attività di creazione dello spazio tramite la luce in cui il pieno è sottomesso al vuoto. Questo vuoto si manifesta attravero spazi stratificati e di transizione che formano una parte importante della consapevolezza dell'abitare nelle regioni tropicali, permettendo anche la percezione simultanea di altri confini spaziali.

Nell'architettura tradizionale dell'Asia sudoccidentale la trasparenza si ottiene senza escludere la privacy e gli spazi protetti. Gli elementi di separazione accentuano la distanza e la differenza; quelli filtranti e di transizione, come pareti, ingressi, scalini e soglie sono rappresentati splendidamente nella ricca architettura tradizionale della regione. Sapientemente utilizzati possono aiutare gli spazi a fluire dall'interno all'esterno in un percorso senza punti di sutura, attirando l'attenzione su soglie e settori intermedi.

A simple shelter is all that is necessary in most covered walkways,
seen above in a house in Singapore.

Un simple techo es todo lo que se necesita en la mayor parte
de las zonas de tránsito cubiertas. Arriba, casa en Singapur.

Basta una tettoia per creare un passaggio coperto,
come in questa casa di Singapore.

Club Med Bali, Indonesia.
Club Med Bali, Indonesia.
Club Med Bali, Indonesia.

«A boundary is not that from which something stops, but, as the Greeks recognised, the boundary is that from which something begins its presencing.»

- Martin Heidegger

«Un umbral no es aquello ante lo que algo se detiene, sino, como ya reconocieron los griegos, el umbral es donde algo empieza a existir.»

-Martin Heidegger

«Un confine non è il punto in cui qualcosa si ferma, ma – come riconobbero i Greci – è il punto da cui qualcosa comincia a manifestare la propria presenza.»

-Martin Heidegger

Regent Chiangmai, Thailand – An architectural stairway acts as a transition area.

Regent Chiangmai, Tailandia – Una escalinata arquitectónica sirve de zona de transición.

Regent Chiangmay, Thailandia – Una scalinata architettonica funge da area di transizione.

House in Singapore.
Casa en Singapur.
Casa a Singapore.

Circulation paths link the indoors to the outdoors.
Los senderos enlazan el exterior con el interior.
Interno ed esterno sono collegati da viottoli.

«They evoke realms that are different yet sharing a common transparency.»

«Evocan reinos que son diferentes aun compartiendo una transparencia común.»

«Evocano regni che sono diversi ma accomunati dalle stesse trasparenze.»

Durchgang innen, Lanna Spa, Chiang Mai, Thailand.
Pasillo interior en el Lanna Spa, Chiang Mai, Tailandia.
Passaggio interno, Terme di Lanna, Chiang May, Thailandia.

PROGRESSION

halls

The hall provides an occasion to gather the impressions of both the interior space as well as the exterior space, and hints at what lies beyond.

PROGRESIÓN

entradas

La entrada proporciona la ocasión de hacerse una impresión del espacio interior y exterior e insinúa lo que hay detrás.

PROGRESSIONE

salone

Il salone permette al visitatore di farsi un'idea dello spazio sia interno che esterno e allude a ciò che si cela «al di là».

A sense of progression suggests an expanse that lies beyond. Space can be manipulated to be expanding or static. A sense of progression can be evoked through a continuous unfolding of changing perspectives, where the viewer experiences the pleasures of containment and revelation. The hall forms an important part of this experience. It provides an occasion to gather the impressions of both the interior and the exterior space, and hints at what lies beyond. Like the transition zone, the hall allows for an intermission along the passage through the spaces.

Una sensación de progresión insinúa el espacio que hay detrás. El espacio puede manipularse para que sea algo en expansión o estático. Una sensación de progresión puede suscitarse a través de un cambio continuo de perspectivas, donde el espectador experimenta los placeres de la contención y la revelación. La entrada es una parte importante de esta experiencia. Proporciona la ocasión de hacerse una impresión del espacio interior y exterior e insinúa lo que hay detrás. Al igual que una zona de transición, la entrada funciona como un entreacto en un pasaje por medio de los espacios.

Il senso di progressione suggerisce l'esistenza di aree «al di là». Lo spazio può essere manipolato al fine di sottolinearne la funzione espansiva o quella statica. La progressione può essere sugerita da uno spiegarsi di prospettive in continuo cambiamento in cui l'osservatore ha la possibilità di provare il piacere del contenimento e della rivelazione. Il salone è una parte importante di questa esperienza; permette di farsi un'idea dello spazio sia interno che esterno e allude a ciò che si trova «al di là». Come la zona di transizione, il salone crea un intervallo nel passaggio da uno spazio all'altro.

«Mobile or immobile, all that occupy
space belong to the domain of
architecture. Architecture
constitutes itself out of space,
limits it, closes it, encircles it.»
                                    - Auguste Perret

«Móvil o inmóvil, todo esto ocupa
el espacio y es parte de la
arquitectura. La arquitectura se
constituye fuera del espacio,
lo limita, lo cierra, lo rodea.»
                                    - Auguste Perret

«Tutti gli elementi che occupano
spazio, mobili o immobili che siano,
appartengono al campo
dell'architettura. L'architettura vive
di spazio, lo limita, lo chiude, lo
circonda.»
                                    - Auguste Perret

The Datai, Langkawi, Malaysia - A richly furnished interior is conducive for rest.

House in Colombo, Sri Lanka, by C. Anjalendran.
A pool in the middle of the living room provides a tranquil setting.

Casa en Colombo, Sri Lanka, por C. Anjalendran.
Un estanque en medio de la sala de estar proporciona un escenario tranquilo.

Casa di C. Anjalendran a Colombo, Sri Lanka.
Una piscina al centro del soggiorno comunica serenità.

Living room of a house at Rebecca Road, Singapore.
Sala de estar de una casa en Rebecca Road, Singapur.
Soggiorno di una casa privata, Rebecca Road, Singapore.

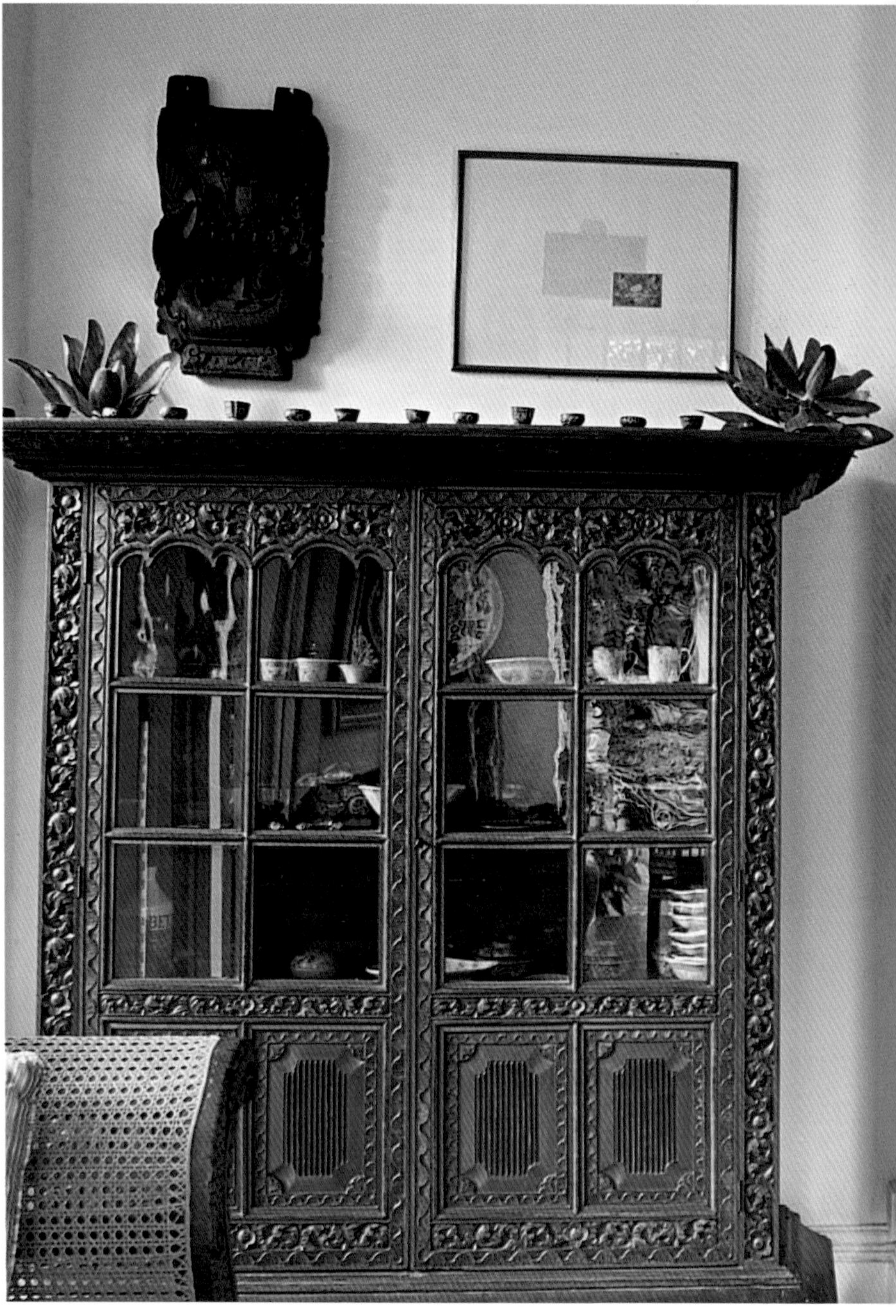

Regent Chiangmai, Thailand – The main living spaces of the suite are split into two levels.

Regent Chiangmai, Tailandia – Los espacios principales de la vivienda están divididos en dos niveles.

Regent Chiangmai, Thailandia – Gli spazi abitativi principali della suite sono distribuiti su due livelli.

A restored colonial house in Singapore.
Una casa colonial restaurada en Singapur.
Casa coloniale ristrutturata a Singapore.

COMMUNICATION

lounges

Spaces for relaxation and contemplation, as well as socialising, must necessarily accommodate both order and flexibility.

COMUNICACIÓN

salones

Los espacios para la relajación y la contemplación, pero también para las relaciones sociales, deben acoger necesariamente tanto el orden como la flexibilidad.

COMUNICAZIONE

soggiorno

Spazi per rilassarsi e meditare, ma anche per intrattenere rapporti sociali, il soggiorno deve necessariamente combinare ordine e flessibilità.

Lounges are spaces for contemplation and relaxation, achieved either through a heightened awareness by a sense of containment, or through a deliberately orchestrated vista of the external world. The materials, colours and textures of furniture and interior finishes are critical in helping to achieve the required sense of relaxation and informality. In traditional Southeast Asian architecture, many lounges are designed as pavilions set in the outdoors. They also form the focus of many resorts and private residences.

Los salones son espacios para la contemplación y la relajación, y ambas se consiguen a través de una clara conciencia del sentido de la moderación, o a través de una perspectiva deliberadamente orquestada del mundo exterior. Los materiales, los colores y las texturas del mobiliario y de los acabados interiores son fundamentales para ayudar a conseguir esta necesaria sensación de relajación e informalidad. En la arquitectura tradicional del sudeste asiático, muchos salones se han diseñado como pabellones que comienzan en el exterior. También son el punto principal en muchos hoteles y residencias particulares.

Il soggiorno è un luogo in cui rilassarsi e meditare; ciò è favorito da un'intensificazione della consapevolezza provocata dal senso di contenimento oppure dalla vista deliberatamente orchestrata sull'ambiente esterno. I materiali, i colori e la struttura dell'arredamento e dei dettagli sono fondamentali per ottenere la sensazione di rilassamento e informalità. Nell'architettura tradizionale dell'Asia sudorientale molti soggiorni sono concepiti come padiglioni situati all'esterno della casa e rappresentano anche il fulcro di molte residenze turistiche e private.

«The important question to ask is not 'what',
but 'how'. What goods we produce or what
tools we use are not questions of spiritual value.»

- Mies van der Rohe

«La cuestión principal que hay que plantearse
no es el 'qué' sino el 'cómo'. Qué artículos
producimos o qué herramientas utilizamos
no son cuestiones de valor espiritual.»

- Mies van der Rohe

«La questione fondamentale non è 'cosa'
ma 'come'. Gli strumenti che usiamo o gli
oggetti che produciamo non hanno alcun
valore spirituale.»

- Mies van der Rohe

Built-in seats along a walkway in Novotel Lombok, Indonesia.

Asientos empotrados a lo largo de un pasillo en el Novotel Lombok, Indonesia.

Sedili incorporati lungo un passaggio coperto, Novotel Lombok, Indonesia.

A shaded pavilion in Amanusa, Bali, Indonesia.

Un pabellón cubierto en el Amanusa, Bali, Indonesia.

Padiglione ombreggiato, Amanusa, Bali, Indonesia.

A private house in Bali, Indonesia.

Una casa particular en Indonesia.

Casa privata a Bali en Indonesia.

A lounge located on the upper storey of a house in Bali, Indonesia.

Un salón situado en el piso superior de una casa en Bali, Indonesia.

Salotto al piano superiore di una casa a Balien en Indonesia.

An intimate pavilion is further defined by lush drapery.

Un pabellón íntimo se puede definir más con un rico drapeado.

Un padiglione reso ancora più intimo dalla vegetazione lussureggiante.

A raised pavilion set amidst a water garden
in Bali, Indonesia.

Pabellón levantado en medio de un jardín de agua
en Bali, Indonesia.

Padiglione rialzato in un giardino sull'acqua
in Bali, Indonesia.

The relationship with the outdoors is cleverly exploited in this private lounge.
La relación con el exterior se aprovecha inteligentemente en este salón particular.
Il rapporto con l'esterno è sapientemente sfruttato in questo soggiorno privato.

A pavilion by the pool overlooks a stunning valley
in this intimate setting in Bali, Indonesia.

El pabellón al borde de la piscina crea un ambiente íntimo
con vistas al espectacular valle en Bali, Indonesia.

Il padiglione sulla piscina crea un ambiente intimo da cui si gode
una vista spettacolare della valle sottostante. Bali, Indonesia.

CONVERSATION

dining spaces

Dining is a communal act. The design of dining spaces must incorporate elements that provide a backdrop to enhance and heighten this experience.

CONVERSACIÓN

comedores

Comer es un acto comunitario. El diseño de los comedores debe incorporar elementos que proporcionen un telón de fondo que realcen y acentúen esta experiencia.

CONVERSAZIONE

sala da pranzo

Generalmente i pasti sono un atto comunitario. La progettazione di ambienti in cui si consumano i pasti deve mirare a creare un ambiente che intensifichi proprio questo aspetto.

Dining spaces are architectural and interior showpieces. In many resorts, they are designed to be part of the interior environment, while relating greatly to the outdoors at the same time. Often raised above the landscape, these spaces allow the diners to enjoy panoramic views of the landscape. In the design of the dining space, furniture, lighting and tableware are also essential in complementing the architectural theme.

Los comedores son piezas interiores y arquitectónicas de valor excepcional. En muchas instalaciones turísticas, estos espacios están diseñados para ser parte del ambiente interior, al mismo tiempo que establecen una perfecta relación con el exterior. Los comedores, a menudo erigidos por encima del paisaje, permiten a los comensales gozar de vistas panorámicas. En el diseño de los comedores, el mobiliario, la iluminación y el servicio de mesa son también elementos esenciales que complementan el tema arquitectónico.

Gli spazi in cui si consumano sono i pasti sono il biglietto da visita di molti complessi turistici, dove sono spesso pensati per essere parte dell'ambiente interno pur essendo strettamente collegati anche agli spazi esterni. Spesso si trovano in posizione sopraelevata rispetto al paesaggio, permettendo ai commensali di godere di una vista panoramica. Arredamento, illuminazione e vasellame sono altrettanto importanti per completare l'effetto architettonico d'insieme.

«I personally enjoy eating in a room
that is open to other activities.»

- Terence Conran

«Personalmente disfruto comiendo
en una habitación abierta a otras
actividades.»

- Terence Conran

«Personalmente amo molto mangiare
in una stanza che è aperta ad
altre attività.»

- Terence Conran

Restaurant at Regent Chiangmai, Thailand.
Restaurante en el Regent Chiangmai, Tailandia.
Il ristorante del Regent Chiangmai, Thailandia.

Poolside dining facilities at Amanpuri, Thailand.
Posibilidad de comer al borde del agua en el Amanpuri, Tailandia.
Tavolo e sedie invitano a mangiare sui bordi della piscina in Amanpuri, Thailandia.

An elaborate table setting under a pavilion
in Tanah Gajah, Bali, Indonesia.

Una mesa dispuesta con mucho detalle en
un pabellón en el Tanah Gajah, Bali, Indonesia.

Una tavola elaboratamente decorata
a Tanaj Gajah, Bali, Indonesia.

(**left and right**) Views of dining areas in Novotel Bali, Indonesia.

(**todo**) Vista de las áreas destinadas a los comedores en el Novotel Bali, Indonesia.

(**tutte le foto**) Sale da pranzo nel Novotel a Bali, Indonesia.

Dining under the stars relives
an old practice in the tropics.

Cenar bajo las estrellas revive
una vieja costumbre de los trópicos.

Cena sotto le stelle, secondo un'antica
tradizione diffusa nelle zone tropicali.

RELAXATION

bedrooms

Invoking associations of calmness, serenity and repose, bedrooms provide the backdrop for contemplative quiescence and the phenomenological experience of simple space inhabitation.

RELAJACIÓN

dormitorios

Los dormitorios despiertan asociaciones con la calma, el reposo y la tranquilidad, y ofrecen el telón de fondo para la inactividad y la experiencia fenomenológica de habitar un simple espacio.

RIPOSO

camera da letto

Associate a sensazioni di calma, serenità e riposo, le camere da letto sono l'ambiente ideale per l'esperienza contemplativa e quella fenomenologica di «abitare lo spazio».

Well-designed sleeping zones invoke associations of calmness, repose and tranquillity. They provide the essential background for contemplative quiescence and the phenomenological experience of space inhabitation. As a retreat for regeneration, the most important piece of furniture here is the bed. The bed frame and fabrics also play important roles in the design. Lighting design and the control of daylight are also critical factors that have to be considered.

Los dormitorios bien diseñados, despiertan asociaciones con la calma, el reposo y la tranquilidad. Ofrecen el telón de fondo para la inactividad y la experiencia fenomenológica de habitar un simple espacio. Como un retiro para la regeneración, el elemento más importante del mobiliario es la cama. El bastidor de la cama y los materiales desempeñan también un papel importante en el diseño. El diseño de la iluminación y el control de la luz diurna son factores fundamentales que deben ser considerados.

Zone sonno ben progettate rievocano sensazioni di calma, serenità e riposo e sono l'ambiente ideale per l'esperienza contemplativa e quella fenomenologica di «abitare lo spazio». Come luogo di ritiro e rigenerazione, l'arredo più importante qui è il letto; i materiali con cui è costruito e i tessuti della biancheria svolgono anch'essi un ruolo importante per l'aspetto complessivo. L'illuminazione e il controllo della luce sono inoltre fattori fondamentali da considerare.

Amanjiwo, Java, Indonesia.
El Amanjiwo, Java, Indonesia.
Amanjiwo, Giava, Indonesia.

Amanpuri Resort, Phuket, Thailand.
El Amanpuri Resort, Phuket, Tailandia.
Amanpuri Resort, Phuket, Thailandia.

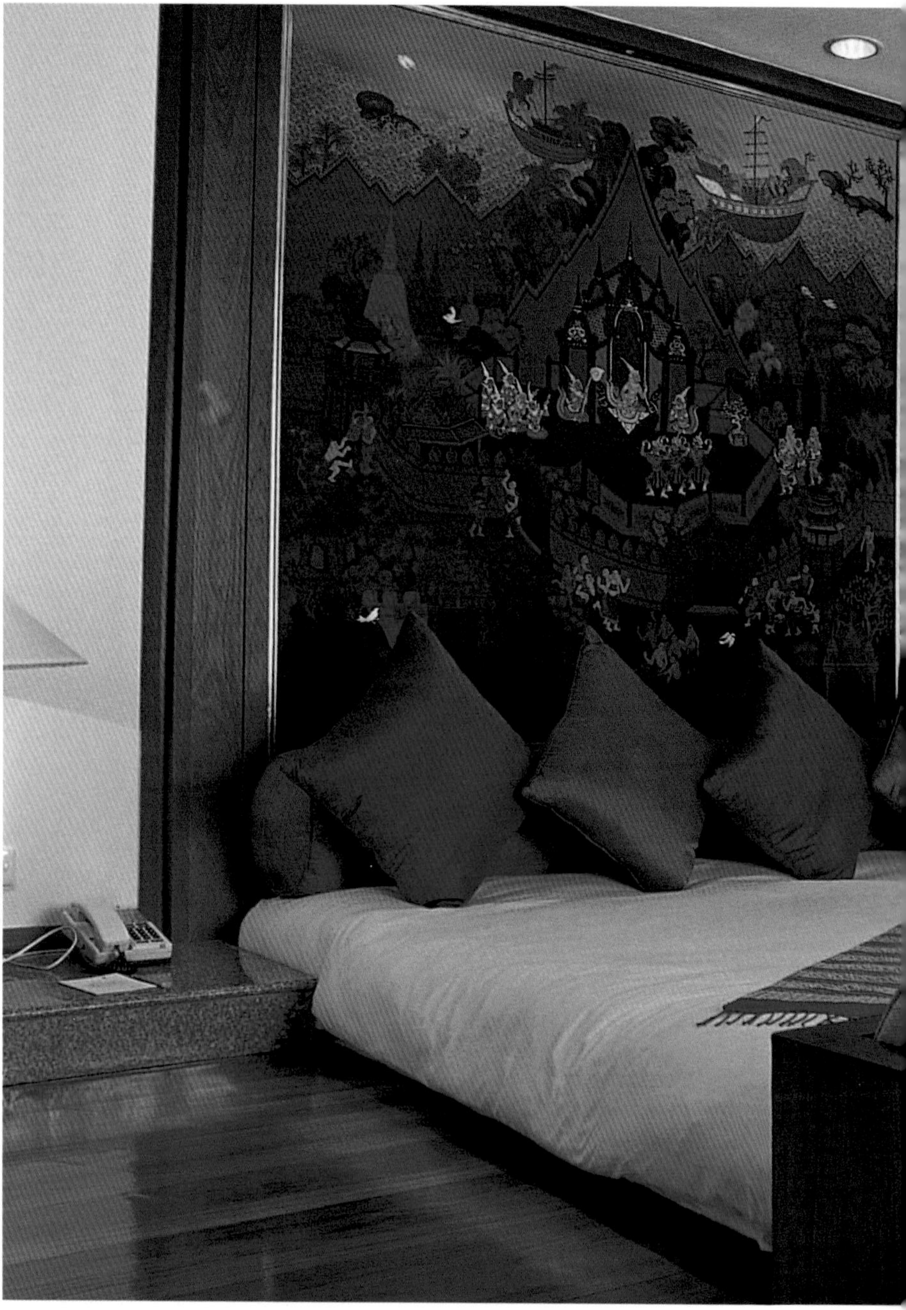

«All good architecture which does not
express serenity fails in its spiritual vision.»

- Luis Barragán

«Toda buena arquitectura que no expresa
serenidad, fracasa en su visión espiritual.»

- Luis Barragán

«Un'opera architettonica che non esprime
serenità viene meno al compito di fornire
una visione spirituale.»   - Luis Barragán

(**left and right**) These rooms are almost spartan, even by Asian standards.
(**todo**) Habitaciones casi espartanas incluso para estándares asiáticos.
(**tutte le foto**) Queste camere sono spartane anche per gli standard asiatici.

The interior of a colonial, «black-and-white» bungalow in Singapore.
Interior de un bungalow «blanco y negro» en Singapur.
L'interno di un bungalow «bianco e nero» a Singapore.

Galle Hotel, Sri Lanka – Designed by Geoffrey Bawa,
the interior is sparsely but tastefully furnished.

Hotel Galle, Sri Lanka – Diseñado por Geoffrey Bawa,
el interior está amueblado parcamente pero con buen gusto.

Galle Hotel, Sri Lanka. L'interno è arredato
in modo parco ma con gusto da Geoffrey Bawa.

CONTEMPLATION

bathrooms

Water is a symbol of purity and meditation. In Asia, it is linked with life. In the home, water is associated with therapeutic qualities and the simple pleasures of bathing.

CONTEMPLACIÓN

cuartos de baño

El agua es un símbolo de pureza y meditación. En Asia se la relaciona con la vida. En el hogar, el agua está asociada con cualidades terapéuticas y con el simple placer de bañarse.

CONTEMPLAZIONE

bagno

L'acqua è un simbolo di purezza e contemplazione. In Asia è associata alla vita. Nell'ambiente domestico l'acqua svolge funzioni terapeutiche e soddisfa il semplice piacere di lavarsi.

The bathroom is a retreat for elemental delights and therapeutic enjoyment. Outdoor baths and showers that open to the skies are increasingly featured. The introduction of plants and light has also opened up what was previously a hermetic box. Combinations of natural materials with their textural contrasts bring out the real luxury of bathing – a heightened sense of touch that is a total surrender to tactility.

El cuarto de baño es un refugio para los placeres elementales y el disfrute terapéutico. Cada vez hay más baños exteriores y duchas a cielo descubierto. La introducción de plantas y de luz ha abierto también lo que antes era una caja herméticamente cerrada. La combinación de materiales naturales y el contraste de sus texturas resaltan el verdadero lujo de bañarse, un sentido del tacto intensificado que es una entrega completa a la apreciación táctil.

Il bagno è un rifugio per soddisfare piaceri elementari e trarne salutare beneficio. Bagni esterni alla casa e docce a cielo aperto si vanno diffondendo sempre più. L'introduzione di piante e luce ha inoltre aperto uno spiraglio in quella che prima era una scatola a tenuta ermetica. Le combinazioni di materiali naturali in tutta la loro varietà rendono ancora più evidente il vero lusso di fare il bagno, arrendendosi completamente al piacere intensificato del tatto.

(**left and right**) Timber wall panelling on a bathroom at Amanpuri Resort, Phuket, Thailand.

(**izquierda y derecha**) Panel de madera en un cuarto de baño en el Amanpuri Resort, Phuket, Tailandia.

(**tutte le foto**) Pannelli di legno in un bagno dell'Amanpuri Resort, Phuket, Thailandia.

Tugu Hotel, Canggu, Bali, Indonesia.
Generous spaces in the bath layout.

Hotel Tugu, Canggu, Bali, Indonesia.
Generosos espacios en la distribución del baño.

Tugu Hotel, Canggu, Bali. Spazi generosi nella
progettazione architettonica del bagno.

Internal courtyard next to the bath.

Patio interior próximo al baño.

Cortile interno vicino al bagno.

An elaborately detailed washbasin.
Un lavabo con detallada decoración.
Lavabo elaboratamente decorato.

PERFORATION

openings

Symbolically, openings are significant because they represent the exposed threshold between the private realm and the public domain.

PERFORACIÓN

aberturas

Simbólicamente, las aberturas son muy importantes porque representan el umbral visible entre el ámbito privado y el dominio público.

PERFORAZIONE

aperture

Le aperture possiedono un alto valore simbolico, poiché rappresentano la soglia esposta tra il regno privato e il dominio pubblico.

The forms of doors, windows and other openings that penetrate solid planes of walls are numerous. Buildings in the tropics typically have a large number of openings to encourage cross-ventilation. Openings function more than merely as openings for entrance and exit, or the admission of light and air. Symbolically, they are significant because they represent the exposed threshold between the private realm and the public domain.

Traditionally, allegorical imagery is incorporated into the design of openings. Rich carvings, gliding and inlays interweave symbolic motifs into the design of these architectural elements. Today, the design of openings is a source of endless variation in materials and colours. They have proved to be a stimulus to architectural imagination.

Las puertas, las ventanas y el resto de las aberturas que penetran en los planos sólidos de los muros pueden adoptar numerosas formas. En las regiones tropicales, por lo general, los edificios cuentan con un considerable número de aberturas para mejorar la ventilación cruzada. Las aberturas funcionan como algo más que meras entradas o salidas o accesos para la luz y el aire. Simbólicamente, son muy importantes porque representan el umbral visible entre el ámbito privado y el dominio público.

Tradicionalmente, al diseño de las aberturas se le añade una imaginería alegórica. Ricos tallados, altorrelieves e incrustaciones se entretejen con motivos simbólicos en el diseño de estos elementos arquitectónicos. Hoy en día, el diseño de las aberturas es toda una fuente interminable de variación en los materiales y los colores, y se ha convertido en un estímulo para la imaginación arquitectónica.

Le forme di porte, finestre e altre aperture che penetrano le superfici solide delle pareti sono varie. Nelle zone tropicali gli edifici dispongono solitamente di un grande numero di aperture allo scopo di favorire la ventilazione. Le aperture non hanno solo la funzione di entrate o uscite o di regolare l'afflusso di aria e luce, ma possiedono un alto valore simbolico, poiché rappresentano la soglia esposta tra il regno privato e il dominio pubblico.

Tradizionalmente, le aperture sono marcate da decorazioni allegoriche. Intagli e intarsi elaborati si intrecciano con motivi simbolici dando forma a questi elementi architettonici. Oggi le aperture sono caratterizzate da infinite variazioni nei materiali e nei colori. Si sono sempre dimostrate uno stimolo alla fantasia degli architetti.

A garden gateway in Bali, Indonesia.
Puerta de un jardín en Bali, Indonesia.
L'entrata di un giardino, Bali, Indonesia.

A wonderfully inspiring courtyard in this Geoffrey Bawa house in Sri Lanka.
Jardín interior maravillosamente sugerente en esta casa de Geoffrey Bawa en Sri Lanka.
Un meraviglioso cortile in questa casa di Geoffrey Bawa nello Sri Lanka.

A framed doorway in a Balinese house.
Puerta enmarcada de una casa balinesa.
Ingresso incorniciato in una casa balinese.

A garden doorway leads to the beach in this house in Bali, Indonesia.
Una puerta del jardín da a la playa en esta casa de Bali, Indonesia.
L'entrata del giardino conduce alla spiaggia in questa casa di Bali, Indonesia.

«Every door is at once a boundary, shutting off one area from another, and also a bond between the inside and the outside.»   - Gretl Hoffmann

«Cada puerta es, al mismo tiempo, una frontera, que aísla una zona de otra, y un vínculo entre el interior y el exterior.»   - Gretl Hoffmann

Bamboo chicks screen the interior of this Thai house that is elevated on stilts.
Unos biombos de bambú ocultan el interior de esta casa tailandesa construida sobre pilotes.
Il bambù scherma l'ingresso di questa casa sopraelevata.

«Ogni porta è allo stesso tempo un confine che separa un'area da un'altra, ma anche un legame tra dentro e fuori.»

- Gretl Hoffmann

A simple framed opening in a private residence in Sri Lanka.

Sencilla abertura enmarcada en una residencia privada en Sri Lanka.

Una semplice apertura incorniciata in questa casa a Sri Lanka.

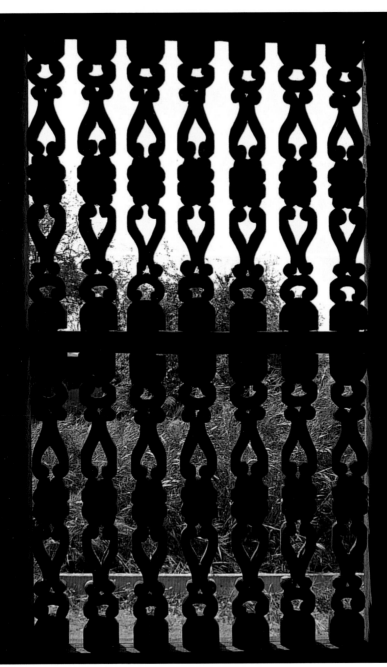

Windows at the end of corridors become part of the interior composition.

Las ventanas al final de los pasillos pasan a integrar la composición interior.

Le finestre in fondo a un corridoio diventano parte della composizione interna.

A central door opens into a generous bathroom
at the Four Seasons Estate in Bali, Indonesia.

Una puerta central da acceso a un amplio cuarto de baño
en el conjunto residencial de Four Seasons en Bali, Indonesia.

Una porta centrale conduce a un grande bagno
nel Four Seasons Estate a Bali, Indonesia.

EXPRESSION

water features

**Man has an instinctive yearning for water in all forms –
still and moving, silent and agitated, therapeutic and sensual.**

EXPRESIÓN

fuentes de agua

**El ser humano siente un anhelo instintivo por el agua en todas sus formas:
en calma y en movimiento, silenciosa y agitada, terapéutica y sensual.**

EXPRESSIÓNE

forme dell'acqua

**L'uomo ha un desiderio istintivo dell'acqua in tutte le sue forme:
ferma o in movimento, silenziosa o agitata, terapeutica o sensuale.**

Water is the ancestral cradle, as well as a source of aesthetic pleasure and therapeutic value. Pleasurable outdoor spaces are incomplete without water, whose primary function is to evoke a heightened awareness of nature. Essential to contemporary landscaping, water receives prominent treatment in gardens as an experiential and reflective element. From fountains to still pools, water offers an alluring effect more powerful than any other feature in the landscape.

El agua es la cuna ancestral, así como una fuente de placer estético y valor terapéutico. Cualquier espacio exterior agradable está incompleto sin agua, cuya función primaria es suscitar una conciencia más clara de la naturaleza. Esencial en la arquitectura paisajística contemporánea, el agua recibe un tratamiento destacado en los jardines como elemento experimental y reflexivo. Ya sean fuentes o estanques en calma, el agua ejerce un efecto seductor más poderoso que cualquier otro elemento del paisaje.

L'acqua è una culla ancestrale oltre che una fonte di piacere estetico e valore terapeutico. Per quanto piacevoli, gli spazi esterni sono incompleti senza l'acqua, la cui funzione fondamentale è di provocare una consapevolezza acuita della natura. Elemento essenziale della moderna progettazione di giardini, l'acqua acquista valore empirico e di riflessione. Dalle fontane alle piscine, l'acqua è in grado, più di qualsiasi altro elemento del paesaggio, di sedurre.

«Water is romantic, sensual, beautiful, happy, strong, sweet, and fresh. Peace and movement, limited and eternal, landscape and architecture, water is life.»

- Ricardo Legoretta

«El agua es romántica, sensual, bella, feliz, fuerte, dulce y fresca. La paz y el movimiento, lo limitado y lo eterno, el paisaje y la arquitectura, el agua es vida.»

- Ricardo Legoretta

«L'acqua è romantica, sensuale, bellissima, felice, forte, dolce e fresca; è pace e movimento, finito e infinito, paesaggio e architettura. L'acqua è vita.»

- Ricardo Legoretta

Club Med, Bali, Indonesia; cascading water features.
Club Med, Bali, Indonesia; fuentes en cascada.
Club Med, Bali, Indonesia; cascate d'acqua.

Club Med, Bali, Indonesia.
Pools form the key feature in the main public space.

Club Med, Bali, Indonesia.
Los estanques son el elemento clave en el espacio público principal.

Club Med, Bali, Indonesia.
Le piscine sono l'elemento chiave nell'area pubblica principale.

(**left and right**) The tranquil and reflective qualities of water are fully appreciated at this swimming pool at Amandari, Bali, Indonesia.

todo) Las propiedades tranquilas y reflexivas del agua se aprecian perfectamente en esta piscina en Amandari, Bali, Indonesia.

(**tutte le foto**) L'elemento di tranquillità e riflessione insito nell'acqua è pienamente espresso in questa piscina dell'Amandari a Bali, Indonesia.

ACCENTUATION

pools and beaches

Water elements, in the form of pools, can be the most compelling design features when carefully set into context with the site and surroundings.

ACENTUACIÓN

piscinas y playas

Los elementos acuáticos en forma de piscinas pueden convertirse en los detalles más decisivos del diseño, siempre que se introduzcan cuidadosamente y en consonancia con las características del lugar y de su entorno.

ACCENTUAZIONE

piscine e spiagge

Elementi acquatici come le piscine possono giocare un ruolo decisivo nel complesso architettonico quando vengono inseriti attentamente nel contesto del luogo e dell'ambiente circostante.

Pools are designed to enhance architecture and its immediate surroundings. Usually incorporated into garden designs, they form compelling features when carefully set into context. A location by the sea also offers a powerful backdrop to any space. Now designed in a staggering number of ways, swimming pools range from free form to austere and Modernist. They are further enhanced by the use of a great number of finishes, ranging from mosaic to glass tiles.

Las piscinas se diseñan con el fin de realzar la arquitectura y su entorno más inmediato. Incluidas por lo general en los diseños de jardines, constituyen detalles decisivos cuando se introducen cuidadosamente y en consonancia con las características del entorno. Un lugar junto al mar ofrece además un poderoso telón de fondo a cualquier espacio. En la actualidad, las piscinas pueden estar diseñadas de un sorprendente número de formas, desde un diseño más libre a otro austero o modernista. Para realzarlas aún más es posible recurrir a un gran número de acabados, ya sea con mosaicos o con azulejos de vidrio.

Le piscine sono progettate per sottolineare la bellezza della struttura architettonica e dell'ambiente circostante. Generalmente inserite in giardini, sviluppano tutto il loro fascino quando vengono inserite attentamente nel contesto. L'ubicazione vicino al mare offre uno sfondo convincente a qualsiasi spazio. Le piscine assumono oggi forme incredibilmente varie, dalla forma libera al modello austero e modernista. Sono inoltre arricchite da una grande gamma di dettagli decorativi dal mosaico alle piastrelle di vetro.

«It is always a question of a problem of attitude between man and his environment, man vis-à-vis the earth, man vis-à-vis the sky, man vis-à-vis the sun – and that, in my opinion, is the true nature of architecture.»

- Mario Botta

«La cuestión es siempre un problema de actitud entre el ser humano y su entorno, del ser humano en relación a la tierra, del ser humano en relación con el cielo, del ser humano en relación con el sol, y esa, en mi opinión, es la verdadera naturaleza de la arquitectura.»

- Mario Botta

«È sempre una questione di rapporto tra uomo e ambiente, tra uomo e terra, tra uomo e cielo e tra uomo e sole: è questa, a mio parere, la vera essenza dell'architettura.»

- Mario Botta

The beach fronting Amanpuri, Phuket, Thailand.

La playa ante el Amanpuri, Phuket, Tailandia.

La spiaggia davanti all'Amanpuri Resort, Phuket, Thailandia.

An infinity-edge pool at Mimpi Resort, Bali, Indonesia.

Piscina con borde horizonte en el complejo turístico de Mimpi en Bali, Indonesia.

Piscina «senza bordo» al Mimpi Resort, Bali, Indonesia.

Novotel Lombok, Indonesia.
Novotel Lombok, Indonesia.
Novotel Lombok, Indonesia.

Mimpi Resort, Bali, Indonesia.
Complejo turístico de Mimpi, Bali, Indonesia.
Mimpi Resort, Bali, Indonesia.

«Give me the luxuries of life and I will willingly
do without the necessities.»　　　- Frank Lloyd Wright

«Que me den los lujos de la vida,
y yo me las arreglaré encantado
sin las necesidades.»　　　- Frank Lloyd Wright

«Datemi qualche lusso e farò volentieri
a meno delle necessità.»　　　- Frank Lloyd Wright

Novotel Lombok, Indonesia – Naturalisitic
pools are integrated with the landscape.

Novotel Lombok, Indonesia – Las piscinas
naturalistas se integran en el paisaje.

Novotel Lombok, Indonesia. Le piscine
naturalistiche sono integrate nel paesaggio.

Mimpi Resort, Bali, Indonesia.

Complejo turístico de Mimpi, Bali, Indonesia.

Mimpi Resort, Bali, Indonesia.

Four Seasons Sayan, Bali, Indonesia.
The pool is located next to the Ayung River in Ubud.

Four Seasons Sayan, Bali, Indonesia.
La piscina está ubicada cerca del río Ayung, en Ubud.

Four Seasons Sayan, Bali, Indonesia.
La piscina è situata vicino all'Ayung River a Ubud.

Novotel Lombok, Indonesia.
Novotel Lombok, Indonesia.
Novotel Lombok, Indonesia.

Multi-tiered pools are common features in Balinese resorts.

Las piscinas con múltiples niveles son elementos habituales en los complejos turísticos de Bali.

Le piscine su diversi livelli sono tipiche degli hotel balinesi.

Pool at Club Med Phuket, Thailand.
Piscina en el Club Med Phuket, Tailandia.
La piscina del Club Med a Phuket, Thailandia.

ANTICIPATION

landscapes and gardens

Plants are used to define space, provide privacy, frame views and create exciting spatial sequences. In the tropics, architecture and landscape are indissoluble.

ANTICIPACIÓN

paisajes y jardines

Las plantas se utilizan para definir un espacio, proporcionar privacidad, enmarcar las vistas y crear emocionantes secuencias espaciales. En los trópicos, la arquitectura y el paisaje son indisolubles.

ANTICIPAZIONE

paesaggi e giardini

Le piante servono a definire gli spazi, rendere intima l'atmosfera, incorniciare viste panoramiche e perfezionare sequenze spaziali. Nei tropici architettura e paesaggio sono elementi inscindibili.

Gardens are an enduring expression of Man's relationship to nature. In the tropics, buildings are not mere objects within the landscape. Shaded gardens provide great relief, whilst plants soften buildings' edges, define space, provide privacy, frame views and create exciting spatial sequences. Delighting through their colours, fragrances, forms and composition, gardens also enchant with their contemplative qualities.

Los jardines son una expresión perdurable de la relación del hombre con la naturaleza. En las regiones tropicales, los edificios no son meros objetos dentro del paisaje. Los sombreados jardines proporcionan un gran sosiego, mientras que las plantas suavizan los bordes del edificio, definen el espacio, aportan privacidad, enmarcan las vistas y crean emocionantes secuencias espaciales. Los jardines no sólo deleitan por sus colores, fragancias, formas y composición, sino que además cautivan por sus cualidades contemplativas.

I giardini sono l'espressione simbolica della relazione tra l'uomo e la natura. Nei tropici gli edifici non sono semplicemente oggetti nel paesaggio. Giardini ombreggiati procurano sollievo, mentre le piante addolciscono gli angoli degli edifici, definiscono gli spazi, rendono intima l'atmosfera, incorniciano viste panoramiche e perfezionano sequenze spaziali. I giardini deliziano con i colori, le fragranze, le forme e le composizioni, ma allo stesso tempo incantano e invitano alla contemplazione.

«A garden is a construction, like a novel by Dostoevsky or Tolstoy. They knew how to capture a climate, to dramatise certain moments, to emphasise. It's the same thing in a garden: how you conduct the spectator to see the same thing from different angles.»

- Burle Marx

«Un jardín es una construcción, como una novela de Dostoievski o Tolstoi. Ellos sabían cómo captar un clima, cómo aportar dramatismo a determinados momentos, cómo enfatizar. En un jardín se trata de lo mismo: de guiar al espectador para que vea lo mismo desde ángulos diferentes.»

- Burle Marx

«Un giardino è una costruzione, come un romanzo di Dostoevskij o di Tolstoj, i quali sapevano come rendere un clima, inscenare e mettere in evidenza determinate situazioni. Lo stesso avviene in un giardino: il tutto sta nel saper condurre l'osservatore a vedere la stessa cosa da angoli diversi.»

- Burle Marx

View of the distant hills at Regent Chiangmai, Thailand.
Vista de las lejanas colinas en el Regent Chiangmai, Tailandia.
Vista panoramica sulle colline dal Regent Chiangmai, Thailandia.

Rice terraces at the Regent Chiangmai, Thailand.
Terrazas de arroz en el Regent Chiangmai, Tailandia.
Terrazze di riso al Regent Chiangmai, Thailandia.

Reflecting pools allow the sky to become
a part of the landscape composition.

Reflejado en las piscinas, el cielo se convierte
en una parte de la composición del paisaje.

Riflettendo il cielo, le piscine lo rendono
parte integrante del paesaggio.

The main pool at Bali Hyatt, Sanur, Indonesia.

La piscina principal en el Bali Hyatt, Sanur, Indonesia.

La piscina principale allo Hyatt di Bali, Sanur, Indonesia.

Waterlily and lotus ponds are commonly used in Bali, Indonesia.

Los estanques de nenúfares y loto se utilizan con frecuencia en Bali, Indonesia.

Stagni di ninfee e loto sono molto diffusi a Bali, Indonesia.

Trees act as screens of privacy.
Los árboles actúan de cortinas que protegen la intimidad.
Gli alberi proteggono la privacy.

Vast expanses of pools define the circulation routes
in many Asian compounds.

Enormes extensiones de piscinas definen los caminos de tránsito
en muchos complejos turísticos asiáticos.

Con le loro ampie superfici le piscine definiscono i percorsi
in molti complessi asiatici.

Rest pavilions serve as architectural counterpoints
in the lush landscape.

Los pabellones de descanso hacen de contrapuntos arquitectónicos
en el exuberante paisaje.

I padiglioni sono elementi architettonici che invitano
al riposo nel paesaggio lussureggiante.

Pergolas provide shade for the pool deck.

Las pérgolas proporcionan sombra sobre la piscina.

Una pergola fa ombra vicino alla piscina.

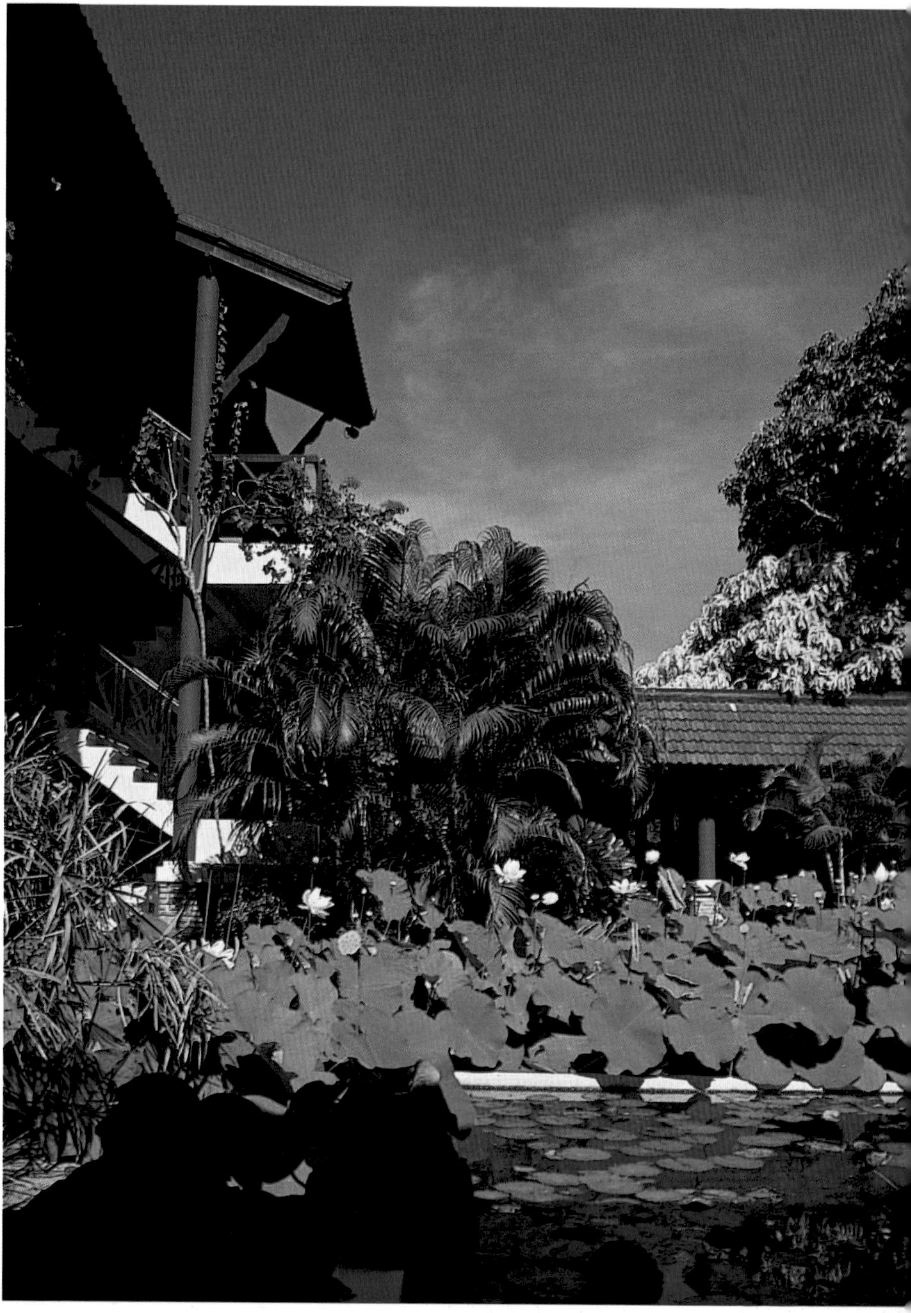

Stepping stones across a lotus pond.

Piedras colocadas para cruzar un estanque de loto.

Passaggio di pietre su uno stagno di loto.

Plants offer privacy to open terraces.
Las plantas ofrecen intimidad a las terrazas abiertas.
Le piante creano privacy su una terrazza aperta.

Private terrace partially screened by plants.

ILLUMINATION

lighting

The poetic fusion of light and space is considered one of the basic tenets of architecture. In tropical Asia, this is further complemented by the richness of effects created by the changing quality of intense light, and the subtraction of such light by architectural elements.

ILUMINACIÓN

luz

La poética fusión entre la luz y el espacio es considerada como uno de los principios básicos en arquitectura. A todo ello se le añade, en las regiones tropicales de Asia, la riqueza de efectos que se crean con las propiedades cambiantes de la intensa luz, y la sustracción de esa luz a través de los elementos arquitectónicos.

ILLUMINAZIONE

luci

La fusione poetica di luci e spazio è uno dei principi fondamentali dell'architettura. Nell'Asia tropicale questa fusione assume varianti del tutto particolari per la ricchezza di effetti creati dalla qualità cangiante della luce intensissima e dalla sottrazione della luce da parte di elementi architettonici.

The poetic fusion of light and space is considered one of the basic tenets of architecture. The manipulation of light and shadow is an important aspect of Asian aesthetic traditions, which extends to achieving a richness of effects through the changing quality of light, and the subtraction of it through the use of architectural elements. Screens are most commonly used to diffuse light and create shadows. Sensitive to nuances of change in the direction and intensity of light, they exhibit a great diversity in finishes and ornamentation. Eave carvings, like those found in Malay, Burmese and Thai architecture, also illustrate the play of shadows in Southeast Asian architecture.

La poética fusión entre la luz y el espacio es considerada como uno de los principios básicos en arquitectura. La manipulación de luces y sombras es un aspecto importante de las tradiciones estéticas asiáticas, que se despliega hasta lograr una riqueza de efectos a través de las propiedades cambiantes de la luz, y la sustracción de ésta por el uso de elementos arquitectónicos. Con mucha frecuencia, se emplean biombos para difuminar la luz y crear sombras. Sensibles a los matices de los cambios en la dirección y la intensidad de la luz, estos elementos presentan una gran diversidad de acabados y ornamentación.
Los tallados en los aleros, como los que pueden encontrarse en la arquitectura malaya, birmana y tailandesa, también ilustran el juego de sombras en la arquitectura del sudeste asiático.

La fusione poetica di luci e spazio è uno dei principi fondamentali dell'architettura. Il gioco di luce e ombra è un aspetto importante delle tradizioni estetiche asiatiche che mirano a ottenere una ricchezza di effetti creati dalla qualità cangiante della luce intensissima e dalla sottrazione della luce da parte di elementi architettonici. Spesso si ricorre a schermi per diffondere la luce e creare ombre. Sensibili a ogni sfumatura di cambiamento nella direzione e nell'intensità della luce, essi mostrano una grande varietà di rifiniture e ornamentazione. Gli intagli nei cornicioni tipici dell'architettura malese, birmana e thailandese illustrano perfettamente il gioco di ombre nell'architettura asiatica sudoccidentale.

Club Med Bali, Indonesia.
Club Med Bali, Indonesia.
Club Med di Bali, Indonesia.

The Rayavadee, Krabi, Thailand.
The Rayavadee, Krabi, Tailandia.
The Rayavadee, Krabi, Thailandia.

«Like the musician's breath in a wind instrument, light and shadow bring out the rich qualities of materials, qualities that remain silent in darkness.»

- Steven Holl

House in Singapore.
Casa en Singapur.
Casa a Singapore.

«Come il fiato di un musicista nello strumento, la luce e l'ombra mettono in risalto le qualità dei materiali, qualità du nell'oscurità rimarrebbero nascoste.»

- Steven Holl

«Como el soplo de un músico en un instrumento de viento, la luz y la sombra ponen de manifiesto las ricas cualidades de los materiales, cualidades que permanecen silentes en la oscuridad.»

- Steven Holl

House in Colombo, Sri Lanka.
Casa en Colombo, Sri Lanka.
Casa a Colombo, Sri Lanka.

Kamandalu, Bali, Indonesia.

Kamandalu, Bali, Indonesia.
Kamandalu, Bali, Indonesia.

Amanpuri Resort, Phuket, Thailand.
Complejo turístico de Amanpuri, en Phuket, Tailandia.
Amanpuri Resort, Phuket, Thailandia.

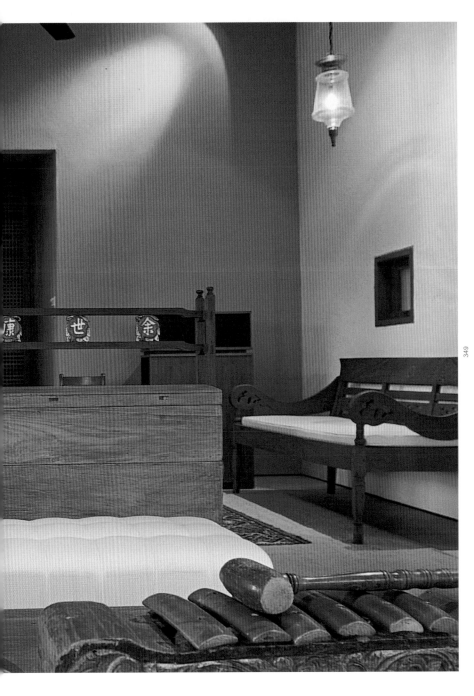

CREATION

art and sculpture

Southeast Asia enjoys a reputation as a veritable paradise for the range of its applied arts, which are closely bound to the religious needs of the people.

CREACIÓN

arte y escultura

El sudeste asiático tiene fama de ser un verdadero paraíso por la variedad de sus artes aplicadas, íntimamente relacionadas con las necesidades religiosas populares.

CREAZIONE

arte e scultura

L'Asia sudoccidentale può essere considerata un paradiso delle arti applicate, strettamente collegate alla vita religiosa delle sue popolazioni.

353

Collections of traditional art and antiques are complementary to the Southeast Asian interior. Exemplified by the ubiquitous Buddha image, they lend an air of contemplative grace to any space. Southeast Asia also enjoys reputation as a veritable paradise for the range of its architectural woodcarvings and applied arts, which are closely bound to the peoples' religious needs and a manifestation of their love for beauty and functional inventiveness. Handcrafted objects of great grace are produced in an amazing array of textures and colours, employing time-honoured traditional skills. Characteristics from the rich artistic traditions of India and China are often also fused with ethnic peculiarities of their folk crafts.

En el sudeste asiático, los interiores se complementan con colecciones de arte tradicional y antigüedades. Ejemplificadas por la omnipresente imagen de Buda, dan un elegante aire contemplativo a cualquier espacio. El sudeste asiático tiene también fama de ser un verdadero paraíso por la variedad de sus tallas de madera y sus artes aplicadas, íntimamente relacionadas con las necesidades religiosas del pueblo y manifestación del amor popular por la belleza y la inventiva funcional. Se fabrican objetos artesanales de una gran elegancia y en un increíble despliegue de texturas y colores, empleando técnicas de larga tradición. Las características de las ricas tradiciones artísticas de la India y China se funden a menudo con peculiaridades étnicas de su artesanía popular.

Le collezioni di arte tradizionale e di antichità sono il naturale complemento degli interni in Asia sudoccidentale. Immagini come quella conosciutissima del Buddha conferiscono un'aria di grazia contemplativa a qualsiasi spazio. L'Asia sudoccidentale può essere considerata un paradiso degli intagli architettonici e delle arti applicate, strettamente collegate alla vita religiosa delle sue popolazioni e manifestazione al tempo stesso del loro amore per la bellezza e della loro inventività sul piano funzionale. Bellissimi oggetti fatti a mano vengono prodotti in una varietà incredibile di forme e colori, utilizzando antiche tecniche tradizionali. Anche elementi del ricco patrimonio artistico indiano e cinese si fondono spesso con particolarità etniche dell'artigianato locale.

367

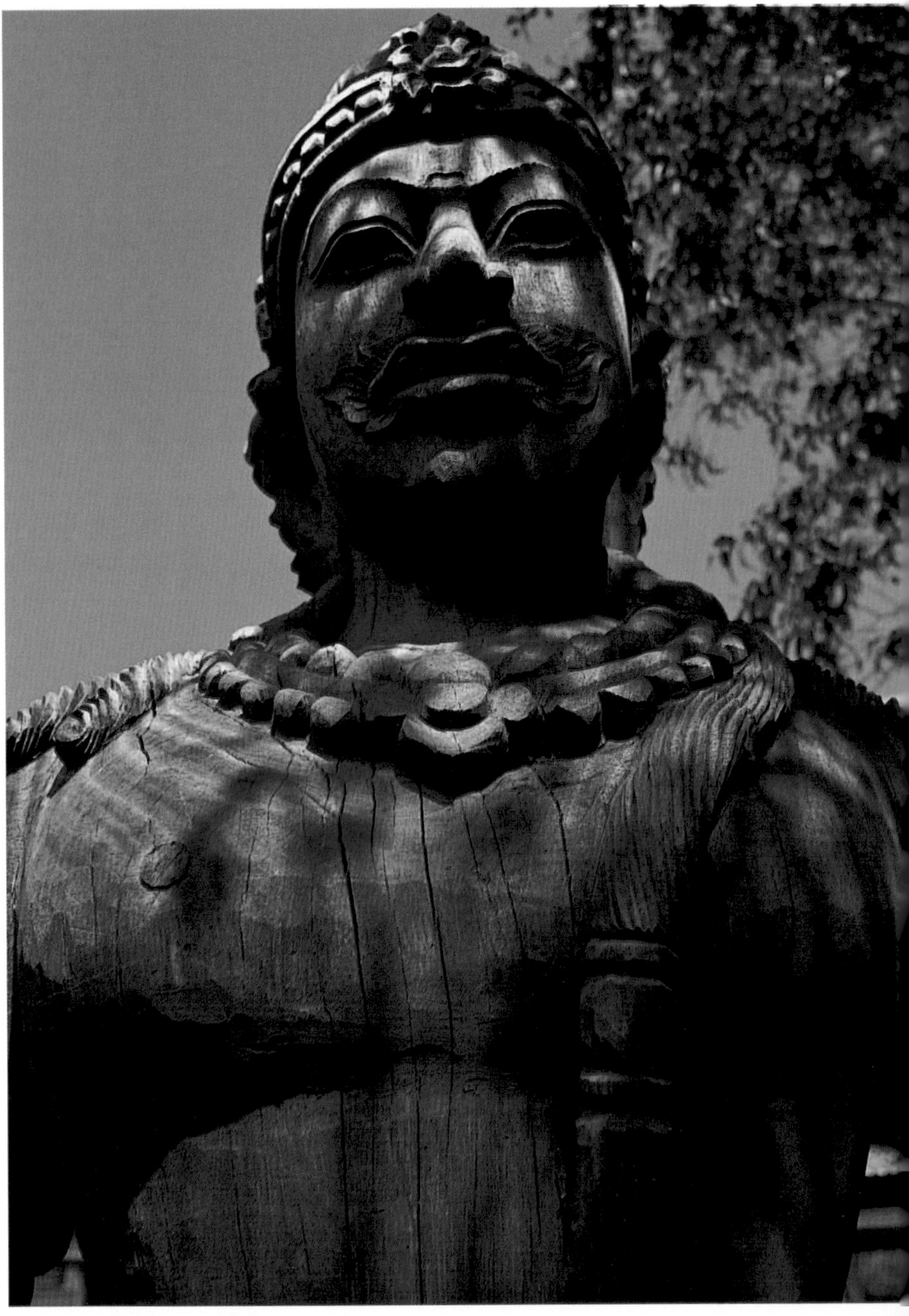

(**all**) Delightful silhouettes of Asian sculptures.
(**todas**) Encantadoras siluetas de esculturas asiáticas.
(**tutte le foto**) Splendidi esempi di scultura asiatica.

Woodcarving placed in an outdoor setting.
Talla de madera ubicada en un espacio exterior.
Scultura lignea in un ambiente esterno.

PROFUSION

details and textures

Art critic Alvar Gonzalez-Palacios has written of his art, «...we recall that the secret of poetry lies not so much in the poetic object as in the heart of the poet who loves.»

PROFUSIÓN

detalles y texturas

El crítico de arte Alvar González-Palacios ha escrito de su arte: «...recordemos que el secreto de la poesía estriba no tanto en el objeto poético, sino en el corazón del poeta que ama.»

PROFUSIONE

dettagli e materiali

Il critico d'arte Alvar González-Palacios ha scritto: «il segreto dell'arte non è tanto nell'oggetto poetico quanto nel cuore del poeta che ama».

The individuality of a building is very much the result of its details. There exists in Southeast Asia a long standing architectural philosophy that sees the relationship between whole and part as crucial to the beauty of a building. The refined proportions of many traditional details create great visual appeal.

Tactile, delectable surfaces can be appreciated by anyone. Materials, in their raw state, stimulate the senses, as well as express the essence of their materiality and age. They are also testaments to the effects of the elements and the passage of time. One of the intrinsic qualities of architecture is the expressiveness of its own nature as constructional elements put together in defiance of gravity. This sense of tectonic quality and tactility, part of what Vitruvius meant by firmitas, is highly developed in the vernacular architecture of Asia.

Inspired by the time-honoured simplicity of traditional Asian architecture and combined with a proclivity for the tactile, many architects practising in the region today are discernibly making a return to the poetic, formal and tactile dimensions of Asian architecture. In the more sensitively designed of contemporary works, a thoughtful and sensual exploration of materials is evident.

La individualidad de un edificio depende en gran medida de sus detalles. En el sudeste asiático existe desde siempre una filosofía arquitectónica que considera crucial la relación entre el todo y la parte para la belleza de un edificio. Las proporciones refinadas de muchos detalles tradicionales crean un gran impacto visual.

Cualquiera puede apreciar las exquisitas superficies táctiles. Los materiales, en su estado más puro, estimulan los sentidos y expresan la esencia de su materialidad y su antigüedad. Son también testimonio de los efectos de los elementos y del paso del tiempo. Una de las cualidades intrínsecas de la arquitectura es la expresividad de su naturaleza propia como reunión de elementos constructivos que desafían la gravedad.

Este concepto de calidad tectónica y tactilidad, parte de lo que Vitruvio denominaba firmitas, está muy desarrollado en la arquitectura típica asiática. Inspirados por la simplicidad consagrada de la tradición arquitectónica de Asia y combinada con una cierta predisposición por lo táctil, en la actualidad, muchos arquitectos de la región están llevando a cabo un retorno a las dimensiones poética, formal y táctil de la arquitectura asiática. En los trabajos contemporáneos, caracterizados por una mayor sensibilidad en el diseño, queda patente una exploración meditada y sensual de los materiales.

L'individualità di un edificio è in gran parte il risultato dei suoi dettagli. In Asia sudoccidentale esiste da sempre una filosofia architettonica che considera la relazione fra la parte e il tutto come elemento cruciale della bellezza di un edificio. Le proporzioni sofisticate di molti dettagli tradizionali esercitano un grande fascino visivo. Superfici gradevoli al tatto possono essere apprezzate da chiunque. I materiali, allo stato grezzo, stimolano i sensi ed esprimono al tempo stesso l'essenza della loro età e struttura materiale. Sono inoltre testimonianze degli effetti degli elementi e del passare del tempo. Una delle qualità intrinseche dell'architettura è l'espressività della propria natura di elementi costruttivi messi insieme sfidando la forza di gravità. Questo legame con la terra e con le percezioni tattili, il che è in parte ciò che Vitruvio intendeva con il concetto di italics, è assai sviluppato nell'architettura regionale asiatica.

Ispirandosi alla semplicità tradizionale dell'architettura asiatica e vivendo appieno la loro sensibilità per l'esperienza tattile, molti architetti attivi in questa regione oggi stanno dichiaratamente tornando alle dimensioni poetiche, formali e concrete dell'architettura asiatica. Nei progetti contemporanei più sofisticati è evidente una ricerca riflessiva e sensuale.

383

«A good building is one that has what
it should have and hasn't got
what it needn't have.»

- Aldo van Eyck

«Un edificio è riuscito quando ha ciò
che dovrebbe avere ma non ciò
che non dovrebbe avere.»

- Aldo van Eyck

«El buen edificio es aquél que tiene
lo que debería tener, y que no tiene
lo que no necesita tener.»

- Aldo van Eyck

Textural contrasts in doorways.
Contrastes de texturas en las entradas.
Materiali a contrasto in un ingresso.

conclusion
conclusión
conclusione

Traditional architecture is a result of the elemental needs of man and his intricate relationships with society and environment. In an era where the real world appears to sublimate into cyberspace, an explicit desire for a return to the past is perhaps understandable. It is critical to examine how significant indigenous archetypes – those that have developed over a long period of time – can be reinterpreted and applied to modern living.

Today, issues concerning the growing ecological consciousness as well as the universalising force of modern architecture and as a manifestation of identity. In Southeast Asia, a growing is seen as a counter-trend towards the universalising force of modern architecture and as a manifestation of identity. In Southeast Asia, a growing number of architects of opposing persuasions have also felt the urgent and irrepressible need for previously neglected cultural introspection and the formulation of national or even regional identities in design. To re-create the traditional in the modern, architects are turning to vernacular architecture as sources for inspiration.

The term «vernacular architecture» is one of the most commonly used but least understood term in the region. Vernacular structures, which are in essence «architecture without architects», provide many basic lessons for architects. These time-proven indigenous shelters were invariably built by anonymous local craftsmen who used local techniques and materials. These indigenous dwellings are well adapted to the extremes of climate and their particular environmental setting, and reflect their society's accumulated wisdom and collective images.

The rejection of the imagistic use of symbols does not imply a rejection of tradition. Architecture contributes to tradition in the process of continual transformation. A number of recent projects in Asia have been strikingly successful in this respect. In Asia, examples of significant regionalist works in different parts of the world demonstrate a high level of collaboration between the architects and the indigenous craftsman.

La arquitectura tradicional es el resultado de las necesidades primarias del ser humano y de sus intrincadas relaciones con la sociedad y el entorno. En una era en la que el mundo real parece sublimarse en el ciberespacio, es quizá comprensible el deseo explícito de volver la vista al pasado. Es fundamental examinar la forma significativa en que los arquetipos indígenas – aquellos que se han desarrollado en el transcurso de un largo período de tiempo – pueden ser reinterpretados y aplicados a la vida moderna. En la actualidad se debate mucho sobre los aspectos relacionados con una mayor conciencia ecológica, así como con la búsqueda ideológica de las raíces nacionales.

El regionalismo actúa como contratendencia frente a la fuerza universalizadora de la arquitectura moderna, y como manifestación de identidad. En el sudeste asiático, un número cada vez mayor de arquitectos de las más diversas tendencias han sentido también la necesidad urgente e irrefrenable de ejercer una introspección cultural, tan olvidada anteriormente, y de proceder a la formulación de identidades nacionales o incluso regionales en materia de diseño. Para recrear lo tradicional en lo moderno, los arquitectos están volviendo a la arquitectura vernácula como fuente de inspiración.

El término «arquitectura vernácula» es uno de los más usados pero menos entendidos en la región. Las estructuras vernáculas, que son en esencia «arquitectura sin arquitectos», proporcionan muchas lecciones básicas a los arquitectos. Estas moradas indígenas probadas en el tiempo eran construidas invariablemente por artesanos locales anónimos que empleaban técnicas y materiales autóctonos. Estas construcciones indígenas están bien adaptadas a los rigores climáticos y a su particular marco natural, y son el reflejo del saber acumulado y el imaginario colectivo de su sociedad.

El rechazo del empleo imagístico de símbolos no implica un rechazo de la tradición. La arquitectura contribuye a la tradición en el proceso de transformación continua. A este respecto, una serie de recientes proyectos desarrollados en Asia han logrado un éxito sorprendente. En Asia, los ejemplos de significativas obras de carácter regionalista en diferentes partes del mundo demuestran un elevado nivel de colaboración entre los arquitectos y los artesanos autóctonos.

L'architettura tradizionale è il risultato dei bisogni fondamentali dell'uomo e dei suoi complicati rapporti con la società e con l'ambiente. In un'epoca in cui il mondo reale sembra sublimarsi nello spazio virtuale, il desiderio esplicito di un ritorno al passato è forse comprensibile. È fondamentale esaminare come gli archetipi indigeni affermatisi nel tempo possano essere reinterpretati e applicati alla vita moderna.

Oggi le questioni riguardanti una crescente consapevolezza ecologica e la ricerca ideologica di radici nazionali si trovano a essere oggetto di vivaci dibattiti. Il regionalismo viene spesso interpretato come una tendenza che contrasta la forza universalistica dell'architettura contemporanea e come una manifestazione di identità. Nell'Asia sudoccidentale un numero sempre maggiore di architetti di tendenze opposte ha sentito l'esigenza urgente e profonda di dedicarsi a un'introspezione culturale precedentemente trascurata e alla formulazione di identità nazionali o addirittura regionali nella loro attività creativa. Al fine di ricreare elementi tradizionali in un contesto moderno, gli architetti hanno cominciato a rivolgersi all'architettura vernacolare come fonte di ispirazione.

Il termine «architettura vernacolare» è molto usato ma poco compreso. Le strutture vernacolari, che sono in fondo «architettura senza architetti», sono lezioni di base per gli architetti. Le abitazioni tradizionali venivano costruite da artigiani locali anonimi che utilizzavano tecniche e materiali locali; si adattavano perfettamente alle condizioni climatiche esterne e al loro particolare contesto ambientale, riflettendo pienamente il bagaglio di conoscenze e l'immaginario collettivo della società che le aveva prodotte.

Il rifiuto dell'uso imagistico dei simboli non implica un rifiuto della tradizione. L'architettura contribuisce a formare la tradizione in un processo di trasformazione incessante. Una serie di progetti recenti in Asia ha riscontrato grande successo sotto questo aspetto; in questa parte del mondo esempi di opere vernacolari dimostrano una collaborazione ad alto livello tra architetti e artigiani indigeni.

bibliography
bibliografía
bibliografia

Shelley-Maree Cassidy, *A Place to Stay*, Conran Octopus Limited, 2000.

David Collins, *New Hotel*, Conran Octopus Limited, 2001.

Kenneth Frampton, *Studies in Tectonic Culture*, MIT Press, 1995.

Paul-Alan Johnson, *The Theory of Architecture: Concepts, Themes & Practices*, Van Nostrand Reinhold, New York, 1994.

Hasan Uddin Khan, *Charles Correa*, Concept Media, Singapore, 1987.

Anthony King, ed., *Culture, Globalization and the World-System*, Macmillan, London, 1991.

David Lowenthal, *The Past is a Foreign Country*, Cambridge University Press, Cambridge, 1985.

Robert Maxwell, *Sweet Disorder and the Carefully Careless*, Princeton Architectural Press, New York, 1993.

Steven Holl, Juhani Pallasmaa, Alberto Perez-Gomez, *Questions of Perception - Phenomenology of Architecture*, A+U Architecture & Urbanism, Tokyo, July 1994.

Juhani Pallasmaa, «Six Themes For The Next Millennium» in *The Architecture Review*, July 1994.

Juhani Pallasmaa, «An Architecture of the Seven Senses» in *Questions of Perception*, A+U Architecture and Urbanism, July 1994 Special Issue.

David Robson, *Geoffrey Bawa: The Complete Works*, Thames and Hudson Ltd, London, 2002.

Ismail Serageldin, *Space For Freedom: The Search For Architectural Excellence in Muslim Societies*, Butterworth Architecture, London, 1989.

Christian Norberg-Schulz, *Genius Loci: Towards a Phenomenology of Architecture*, New York: Rizzoli International Publications, Inc., 1980.

Tan Hock Beng, *Tropical Architecture and Interiors*, Page One Publishing Pte Ltd, Singapore, 1994.

Tan Hock Beng, *Tropical Resorts*, Page One Publishing Pte Ltd, Singapore, 1995.

Tan Hock Beng, *Tropical Retreats: The Poetics of Place*, Page One Publishing Pte Ltd, Singapore, 1996.

Tan Hock Beng, *Tropical Paradise*, Page One Publishing Pte Ltd, Singapore, 2000.

Jun'ichiro Tanizaki, *In Praise of Shadows*, translated by Thomas J. Harper and Edward G. Seidensticker, Charles E. Tuttle Company, Inc, Tokyo, 1990.

Brian Brace Taylor, *Geoffrey Bawa*, Concept Media, Singapore, 1986.

photo credits
créditos fotográficos
crediti fotografici

All photos by Tan Hock Beng except those listed below:

075 Bill Bensley
122 Bill Bensley
144-145 Grahacipta Hadiprana
200-201 Hotel Tugu, Bali
202-203 Waka Group
259 Bill Bensley
263 Bill Bensley
268-269 Bill Bensley
274 Bill Bensley
277 Bill Bensley
284-285 Bill Bensley
340-341 Yori Antar / courtesy of Andra Matin
378-379 Jimmy Lim

acknowledgements
agradecimientos
ringraziamenti

This collection is essentially an expansion of Tropical Architecture and Interiors, first published in 1994, which originally set out to be a simple collection of some of the several thousands of images that the author had taken while travelling around Asia. The incredibly rich region has provided the most sublime stage-sets for human drama, and its encompassing poetics of built-forms. This collection continues to add to the increasing body of literature and imagery of tropical design.

Many people have shared their time and profound knowledge with me. Their advice, support and friendships have been invaluable. Many of my trips were made much easier and less stressful by all the staff in my studio, especially my office manager Lenny Wiria Wibowo and my personal assistant Lizzy Lim. This book was being produced at the same time as Pleasures of Resort Living. Hence, I am thankful to the same group of people who have helped me complete two books simultaneously. Foremost on my list, I would like to thank my publisher, Mark Tan, who once again initiated the early ideas, and persuaded me to continue working on the book despite my busy schedule, as well as my editor, Kelley Cheng, designers and writers Jacinta Neoh, Wong Chai Yen, Ang Hwee Chuin and Selina Lim - all from Page One Publishing - for doing what they do so well. They are the crucial underpinning to the book. I also owe special gratitude to Bill Bensley, Jirachai Rengthong, Brian Sherman, Lek Bunnag, Louisa Bunnag and Melvyn Goh. Others provided platforms and support. They include Paiboon Damrongchaitam, Winita Wiranaruk, Heng Lee Kwang, William Lim, Lena Lim, Kwok Kian Woon, Jonathan Moult, Ines Noe, Karan Grover, Kerry Hill, Rolf Hubner, Sunshine Wong, Michael and Michaela Muller, Dino Barre, Sinatra Arto Hardy, Ken Yeang, Anura and Sundarika Ratnavibhushana, Andra Matin, Jimmy Lim, Indra Leonardi, Everett Dowling, Mei Lee Wong, Brian Ige and Don Fujimoto. I wish also to extend my particular gratitude to many others who have helped in making my trips and photography sessions so much easier and enjoyable. Among these, particular credit should be accorded to Bill Heinecke, Lee Sutton, Royal Rowe, Putu Indrawati, Rainata Tjoa, Christine Galle, Edwin Yeow, Maisy Koh, Ilkin Ilyaszade, and Ketut Siandana. Most of all, my gratitude goes to my family: Maria, Brent and Gale. They have, as always, been the powerful leading forces behind each book's completion.

Tan Hock Beng | Singapore, November 2002

Esta colección es, en esencia, una ampliación de la obra Tropical Architecture and Interiors, publicada por primera vez en 1994, que en un principio se proponía ser una sencilla recopilación de algunas de las miles de imágenes tomadas por el autor mientras viajaba por Asia. La increíble riqueza de la región ha proporcionado los escenarios más sublimes para el drama humano, además de la poética que se desprende de sus formas constructivas. La presente recopilación supone una contribución al número cada vez mayor de publicaciones e imágenes en torno al diseño propio de las regiones tropicales.

Son muchas las personas que han compartido conmigo su tiempo y sus profundos conocimientos. Sus consejos, su apoyo y su amistad han sido incalculables.